Sowing

The Increasing Years

The second account in the inspirational
Relinquish & Reap Series
by

Jessica Janna

&

April Alisa Marquette

April Rain Books

Sowing
© Copyright 2010 by A Rain Worx
Edited by D. Niecy
yniecy@verizon.net

ISBN 978-1-61539-574-3

Printed in the United States of America

Some of the names in this narrative have been changed.

Visit the author at www.aprilalisamarquette.com
Library of Congress Catalog Card No.: On File

Dear Reader,

I wanted to share something with you.

I chose the hollyhock, the flower that graces the cover, for its beauty and for its resilience. Although it is a popular ornamental plant, it's also drought resilient, and does well in full sun –a location that often times causes other plants to wilt. This particular species lives a number of years, and acquires many descendants.

I'll tell you, I also chose the hollyhock because it reminds me of the human spirit. Beautiful and resilient, many of us have come through droughts—times in our lives that have been fraught with tension and perhaps even tears. Many may have lived in locations where others surely would have wilted, or failed. Yet we have made it, for any number of years, truly by the grace of God, and many of us have acquired descendants.

Today, I urge you to look at the beautiful resilient hollyhock, or even at other flowers. Then I suggest that you think of yourself. Afterward smile, and go on, in the knowledge that yours is a life of purpose. Yours, like mine, is, and can further be, a life of reaping. Yes, when old things, hurtful things, ugly things are not wallowed in, but given up, relinquished... Give and get.

Relinquish and reap,

Jessie

Be strong and take heart, all you who hope in the Lord.

Psalm 31:24

Table of Contents

Table of Contents
Cont'd

Now a Youngling

I was about twelve years old, a youngling, no longer a *Seedling*, when a cousin in Chicago wrote to my mother asking if my older sister would be able to visit her. My cousin wanted this because she needed help with her small children during the summer. Although they would be out of school, she would yet have to work. Therefore, she needed someone to look after them.

My mother, Ms. Cleo, said my sister could not go. Sister was newly married. She was also in college, and had a new baby. However, Mother did say that I could go. She told me about the opportunity. Listening, I remembered my cousin.

Older than I was, she'd lived in Tennessee at the same time that we did. She had since moved to Chicago. However, my cousin, a beautiful brown woman, with a lovely head of thick healthy hair had always been fond of me. When I'd been a little thing, Cousin and her husband, a great-looking couple, had carried me to shows, and to the circus.

Therefore, knowing she needed help, I wanted to go, especially since Sister could not. Somehow, I felt like it was my time, at last.

I told you, while recounting my youngest years in *Seedling*, that for longer than I could remember, I'd wanted a different life. Often as a seedling I'd prayed for a way out of Arkansas' forever fields of cotton. I hated the chopping, the hoeing, the picking and planting. I wanted away from the pitch black nights, the army worms, and the bugs. I abhorred that seemingly endless, oh so tiresome life of cultivating the soil. Therefore, when Cousin called, as an adolescent I felt like that was God's way of getting me out. I would finally get out of Pine Bluff, I thought, and away from Grandmaw who had often taunted me. I felt as if the road was being prepared just for me.

Sweet Mother

During this time, Mother, who had always been busy, was at home. There, she did all that she always had, to keep home and hearth together. She would yet rise before the sun, to pray while she marched around creating order and beauty. While she fixed breakfast, she would also use her thin, high soprano voice to sing of her wondrous God. She would start the wash, and sweep the walk. She'd pick and begin to snap beans for a later meal. She would rouse the family, and keep everything and everyone moving, before she would somehow find time to mend, and make lovely lace-trimmed sheets, pillowcases, and clothing for her children.

She grew corn, cucumbers, tomatoes and okra, among other things.

Now some of you may remember Pretty, the baby that we lost in *Seedling*. Well, after Pretty, Mother found herself expecting again. Born in Pine Bluff, this time the infant, Baby Sister, lived. Mother wondered what to name the new baby. The family tried out a few names, and I happened to suggest a name I liked. I'd known a girl at school who was quite lovely, from the inside out. I felt her name fit her. Therefore, I suggested her name to Mother. The family added a middle name and Baby Sis got her moniker!

I didn't take care of Baby Sis though, like I'd done Brother, because he and I were actively going to school by the time Baby Sis came along. Also, after having married E G, Mother was able to stay home with the new baby. Sure, Mother worked planting, washing, canning, cooking, sewing, mending and the like, but she no longer had to go to a field to get cheated by a Mr. Boss Man. She was able to spend time with the baby—more than she had with her elder children. Baby Sis quickly grew, and I got to spend more time with Mother.

I recall having many a dream. In one I remember being in a large field, running. Lighting was striking on every side, and fearful, I ran harder. When I woke, frightened, I asked, "Mother, what could that mean?"

Calmly, as was her way, she simply said, "God is trying to get your attention. He wants you."

Hearing that I asked, "What do I have to do?"

"Just say yes."

I'll never forget; I started crying then because I so wanted to know God. I fell over on sweet Mother who began to pray. Clasping her little hands together, she said a simple prayer, and believing with all my heart, I felt the Holy Spirit that day as it came upon me, to fill me with a shining peaceful presence.

Grandmaw Graduated

At home, Grandmaw was yet sometimes pain-in-the neck-y. Occasionally, she still picked on me, I felt. Yet she left me alone more often than she had in the past. Remember, I also told you that back then people called her Injun, or Indian, but now we know that she was Native American. I also told you that she became my granny when Mother married the tall handsome E G.

Well, by the time I was an adolescent, Grandmaw's hair was no longer dark. For a while she'd had sprinkles of white throughout. Then slowly her long hair progressed, to become totally white. Oh she still wore her two long braids, with the part down the middle. Now though, sometimes she would wear one long white plait that hung like a heavy rope, down her back. Other times she would make a loose bun on the back of her head. Those were her dressed up times, times when she went to what she called *The 'Sociation* in Noble Lake, or some other place in the back woods.

Grandmaw's association stuff was where a number of churches gathered, back in the woods where she had once lived. Yes, back before her husband, the black man, had killed himself. I never knew why Grandmaw's husband did that. It wasn't really spoken of. I do know though, that the man did the deed long before we became a family.

I also know that at that house in the back woods, the one that Grandmaw still owned, there were acres upon acres of farmland. There were horses and cattle too. My step-father E G also yet planted corn, cotton, and other things back there. It was why we went there, to pick cotton, to chop it, or to do some other chore that I detested.

I will never forget that Grandmaw's old house was wooden, with a tin top. Inside the house there were wooden floors—that were blood stained. Those eerie looking stains would always materialize. They would slowly become visible, whenever it rained. We were told that those stains were from the suicide.

For some reason I was never afraid that Grandmaw's husband's ghost would meet us there. I just never liked going there. However, often when we picked cotton, the family and whoever else was working, would go into the house to eat lunch, because the house provided shade. However, whenever we went there, Grandmaw did not. She remained in Moscow, Arkansas.

But back to Grandmaw's meetings that she got dressed up for. I believe they were the Baptist Association meetings. In order to go, she would put on a wide brimmed hat, or she'd wear a pillbox hat. One or the other she would perch atop her head while her hair bun remained at her neck.

I must admit, when she got dressed, Grandmaw could look nice, sort of like the women in that movie that I like, *Sense and Sensibility*. Of course she would powder her little cream colored face. She would also stick a hat pin in her hat. Long, the decorative pin she would push through the felt or the straw of her hat, and through strands of her lengthy hair. Then she'd push the pin out of the other side of the hat, thus, securing it to her head. She would also have her Sunday go-to-meeting clothes and her spool heel shoes on.

I've got to tell you, by this time, little wiry Grandmaw had graduated, to sleeping with a gun—a .45 under her pillow. She groused that she was not going to let anybody come in on her, before she also spoke of a report she'd heard on the news. It said that prisoners had broken out of the Cummings penal system, and the roustabouts were allegedly hiding in ravines, behind bushes, and crossing rivers. Since it seemed they were continually eluding the authorities, pistol-packing Grandmaw said she was going to take care of herself.

In the daytime, she wore long dresses, lace-up oxford shoes, and her braids. She also kept her gun in the house. Often it lay in a tray, in a huge trunk with a heavy lid, so that the kids wouldn't get to it. But if Grandmaw felt scared, which she must have, often, she slept with her 'friend' the gun.

When it was cold out, she would still do what she had when I'd been a seedling. Grandmaw would give me, and my siblings, hot toddies—sugared hot water, spiked with white-lightning, her and E G's homemade whiskey. Oh, she always kept a little jug of liquor beside her bed. Yes and she kept dipping-snuff in her bottom lip. You could see it when you looked her way. The snuff formed a little lump below her lip; and she would spit too, in a coffee can, or a bleach container with the top cut off.

My little wiry no nonsense gun-toting Grandmaw used to also sit on the front porch. In her rocker, she would smoke a pipe, once a month. I don't know what the once a month business was about, but I think she figured it was for good luck.

I have to tell you. For some reason I was no longer experiencing the same amount of kid-animosity toward Grandmaw that I once had. Perhaps it was because I was learning her. I believe I was growing to understand her. Mind you now, she was yet a handful of trouble, to me, sometimes. However she was also helpful, some of the time. She showed me things, and told me others that I yet carry with me, to this day. Therefore, I'll say that in my mind, Grandmaw graduated, from foe to friend.

Often she would tell me to wash my face, by cupping water in my hands, and carrying that water back off my cheeks. She also told me not to pull my skin downward, or, she said, I would look old.

Grandmaw once showed me an elderly woman, one whom Gran swore looked like she had a pile of worms in her face. Grandmaw said so because the woman's skin happened to be quite wrinkled. So, I supposed, she didn't want me looking old, prematurely.

My little pistol packer also told me to close my mouth. Often when she got on my nerves she advised me not to poke out my lips. She told me pouting wasn't pretty. She said I'd get a big mouth

and become ugly, and I believed her.

Experiencing God

As a kid, often I kept to myself. I wrote poems and little songs that I sang under my breath. Then as an eleven and twelve year old, I began to go to church meetings with a bunch of other kids. There was one meeting in particular. It was held at the old church that my family attended. The church was made of grey stone, before it burned; but at this meeting of which I speak, God met us there. I could feel His presence. It was why I was eager to go with the other youngsters whenever there was another meeting in town. I was unaware of it at the time, but I was actively seeking God. I was searching for Him the best way I knew how.

Now there was a Catholic Priest who would come into town for weeks at a time. He would hold healing services, meetings in a large hall. People would travel there, coming from miles around, to be healed. I recall a woman who was obese. She also appeared quite sad, as if her life had been all hardship and tears. At the meeting it was said that she was dying of something. I recall she got healed. I know because weeks later, that same woman returned to the meeting, and her weight had been reduced. She had gone down considerably, and as a youngling I could hardly believe it!

There was also a newsletter circulating, about people who had received healing. There were people in wheelchairs, and they got out of them. There were, of course, other people who had all kinds of stories to tell about the people who'd gotten out of the chairs. These story tellers were perhaps non-believers. They said mean, derisive things, but searching for the divine, they were the people that I ignored.

As youngsters, my friends and I were astounded at that healing presence in the meetings. Being there I saw the virtue of healing flowing all around me. I realize, now, that the people in those meetings took the things that my mother had once taught me, and expanded upon them. Those people, those believers went further. They delved deeper into the spiritual things that I desired to know of.

I also attended other meetings. These were run by a world renowned evangelist. Other youngsters and I were once in the prayer area at an auditorium where this evangelist appeared. People were lined across the altar, and those all around me were collapsing, under the unction of the Holy Spirit. I did not expect to be one of those who fell, but I did. That was amazing to me! I did not get hurt. However it was awesome to feel that type of power, when for so long I had seen it, but had not known it like that.

I would love to explain, to help people to know and understand exactly what I felt, but it is inexplicable really. It simply seemed as if I'd collapsed. My bones and my body just folded, under that wonderful rush.

Being in those meetings, and watching, hearing and experiencing God's power… That was truly amazing to me. Usually I was awed. I stared, with my hands clasped. I was inspired. I wanted to know this God, this being who cared about people. I began to write what little I knew about Him on paper. This I kept to myself. It was my secret.

I thought about God, and about people who weren't all that special. Many were simply hard workers. Some were teachers, some spent time in the fields, others did whatever—I don't know. All I knew was that the something within me that was spiritual began to call out to that something outside of me that was spiritual too. Then I yearned to know more, to better to get to know this God. I was curious about Him, and since my interest in spiritual things had been sparked when I had been a seedling, I desperately needed to understand.

Therefore, at about this time in my life I began to earnestly pray. I'd always prayed, from a little girl, but no longer was I praying the baby prayers that I had once been taught. I began to truly and sincerely seek God.

Whiskey Still

While I was at home singing, praying, and
attempting to learn of the God of the Universe, all
while helping my mother by doing chores,
Grandmaw and E G tended their business. In the
back woods they made White Lightning. Then E G
supplied it to his customers. Yes, my family
members were still making their own liquor and
profiting from it. Often they went back there to tend
their venture. They had it deep in the woods so the
authorities wouldn't get onto them.

Back in the trees, they made liquor out of corn
that fermented in big containers. It was called sour

mash, and this liquid would then travel through the pipes of the distillery. It was really some operation.

For unknown reasons, the police didn't often trail E G. Not when he made deliveries to his various customers. They didn't bother him either, when he frequented the tin roof jook-joints, sort of like a traveling salesman.

From those kinds of places, music, honky-tonk and guitar licks, like those of B.B. King and whatever other blues man of the day, loudly streamed out. Gussied up women would stagger or teeter, giggling, out of those places with their high heels on. Spiffed up men strolled about, smoking.

Often, Mother's tall, handsome E G would stand outside those jook-joints and shoot his pistol up into the air. He would watch then as the remaining club patrons quickly poured out of those establishments and onto the street, like bats converging on mosquitoes. Panicked, screaming and hollering, those nervous club patrons would then become prime targets to whom E G could offer his wares.

Clean and Unclean

Now that I was actively seeking to know God and his mysteries, I began to have dreams. These did not create fear in me; they just allowed me to know that the God that I was seeking sought me too.

I began to pray more often, even for family members and others. I subsequently began to feel as if healing was in my hands. I mentioned this to my mother, and my bookworm sister stood there, scowling. She must have thought I was trying to get 'above myself' because she burst out with a question. She asked, "How can a clean thing come out of an unclean thing?"

By that she was saying, how could God reside in *me* —when I came out of Mother who was no notable God-woman? That assumption both angered and hurt me, *but* it did not deter me from seeking. I was on a quest, and I was not about to let some little mean-spirited words derail me. Also, in her soft way, Mother encouraged me and I have since realized that if one is going to do anything in life, they may also have to overcome the words, jibes, and sneers of others. That is just how things are, sometimes.

Beginning the Journey

Well, by the time my cousin called again, my
fare was paid. Finally, I left for Chicago, to care for
Cousin's children over the summer. By that time I
think Baby Sister was about ready to start school.
Leaving her and the family behind, I journeyed by
train. It stopped in St. Louis. So I got to visit with
two of my Aunts. One we called by her nickname,
and she was the cutest thing. She was the mother of
my cousin in Chicago, the one whom I was on my
way to visit and help. My next train, or it could
have been a bus—it's been so long since that trip—
left that evening.

However, before it did, while spending time
with extended family, things were said, about me.

My cousins oohed and ahhhed. They said, "She doesn't talk like she's from the south." They also said, "She has a perfectly round face."

When at last I arrived in Chicago, my cousin's husband and their small son met me at the station. At their home, I met the baby that I would take care of. The small family lived in what was known then as a court way building, perhaps because the structure was shaped like a U. It had apartment homes on three sides of a courtyard, and inside there were high ceilings and nice wood floors.

During that summer, I also took care of small Son, whom I already knew, and loved. Since he was small, and I was the older cousin, he shyly whispered that I was pretty—which was not bad for my budding adolescent ego. He also cooked up small schemes whereby his little school friends could see me, like I was a movie star or something. I'm tickled to recall it. My cousin's baby was sweet too, and he grew to love me. Oh, was it a joy to see how excited he became whenever he saw me! And I must say I was good and sweet to both of those children.

When the baby began toddling, he would enter the room that I shared with small Son. Baby would kiss my feet and in his little broken language, he'd tell me he loved me. Wow, does telling you this bring back memories... It almost makes me cry because I believe that was the first time that I truly felt precious, to anyone. I tell you, small children have a way of bringing out the best in a person, if it's there.

At my cousin's nice flat, I remember there being two bedrooms. I did not have my own room, but it did not bother me. I was just happy that I was no longer in Arkansas, fighting rats in the night. I was no longer frightened of what was out in the cotton fields. At Cousin's house in the city, I slept on a cot, in her small son's room, and there, my surroundings were quiet, most of the time.

Over the course of that summer I felt okay. Then when the fall arrived, there were changes. Instead of me being shipped home, it had been arranged, without my knowledge. I would go to school, in Chicago. This Cousin had worked out with Mother. Although at the time it was not a bad thing; to me, a child, it felt like no one at home wanted me. I felt as though no one had asked for me to return. That hurt, and smarted in places that I

didn't even realize were wounded…

The Stirrings of Trouble

I don't know if I mentioned that my cousin
worked in a beauty salon, and sometimes she
worked late hours. A few times she did my hair, and
after all these years I can only guess that it looked
nice. I cannot remember, probably because at that
age, I really didn't give my looks much thought. I
do remember that Cousin was a beautiful woman
with thick long heavy hair and olive-skin. As a
child, I adored her and her husband. They were a
lovely couple who had only been nice to me. They
had taken me, and their children, to the World's
Fair. We'd also enjoyed rodeo shows, and merry-
go-rounds.

I can't remember Cousin paying me to babysit though, perhaps because she was housing me, but she did see to me having money to go to school. Later, people even gave me clothes, lots of necessary warm things. I believe these people were friends of Cousin's. Some may have even been her salon patrons. The clothing I received included ruffle-sleeve dresses and used but nice baby clothes.

By this time, I'd been in Chicago a good while and sent some of what I received home, thinking Mother could use those things for my siblings. Yet I took care of my small cousins, in the evenings after I came in from school. They sat around me and played, while I would do my homework. Then their father would come home from work to cook. If not, he would heat up the meals that my cousin, his wife, had previously prepared. On other nights she would get home early enough to fix dinner.

I began to notice undercurrents. I'd previously lived through enough trouble to be able to recognize them. Therefore I knew when my cousin and her husband hissed and fought. It seemed that when he got paid, one of two things would happen. One, she would leave her work to go up to his job to retrieve his pay. Two, if she was unable to do so, that was the end. Husband and his so-called buddies would drink up his pay. Thus, Cousin would become very angry, and subsequently there were fights.

Nowadays, I wonder if those 'buddies' only drank up my cousin's husband's pay. I wonder if they carried their own home.

A Terrifying Experience

I heard Cousin speak with her girlfriend about the drinking/pay situation. Now I must tell you. Girlfriend's man happened to be one of the dreaded drinking buddies, and most likely without her knowledge, drinking buddy started frequenting my cousin's home, usually when Cousin and her husband were not there.

One particular day this man appeared and was drunk. I did not want to let him in, but he claimed he would just wait for my cousin's husband. As an adolescent, I really had no idea what to do. I knew someplace deep within that the situation felt wrong. Therefore, since I'd been coerced into allowing the drinking buddy into the apartment, I tried to stay out of his way. I attempted to keep the little ones I was in charge of away from him too.

Yet he found me, and tried to force himself on me. He wrestled to kiss me, and frightened, I wrangled to keep away from him. However, he managed to put his smelly mouth on my skin. Forcefully, he kept attempting to kiss and pin me down, but as thin and as young as I was, I struggled and fought. I knew enough from my past to know that he would do something painful to me; and as it was, he was hurting and frightening me something awful, so I pushed him, with everything I had. Then while shaking with fear, and nearly erupting with sobs, I hit him. With what I don't remember, but it was near to hand and I grabbed it, just wanting him to stop, to disappear, to go away forever. I guess I must have knocked his drunk self down, or he lost his balance—whichever way it happened, he fell.

I didn't realize, until I began to tell you, that this was buried deep in my psyche. Of course I knew it was a memory, something I'd experienced, but previously I had not realized how deeply it had affected me. To be honest, I really didn't want to go into this. I was ashamed; but why should *I* be ashamed? I did nothing wrong—save for allow that lout into my cousin's home. However, I was a child! I hadn't been told to bar him from the abode. Also, I had been raised to be respectful, to adults, so that drunken lousy adult thought to take advantage of me. It just became one more secret for me to carry, and secrets of that kind become heavy. They weigh a person's spirit down. Therefore, when the

adults returned home, I made myself scarce. I
simply wanted to become invisible. I wanted to
hide. It is a feeling that I had become very familiar
with, perhaps because during the course of my
young life, I had never truly felt safe.

Seeking Solace

Back then, whenever I sought solace, it was in church, just as I had back when I lived in Arkansas, but now Mother wasn't around to take me. While living in Chicago, to attend church, I had to travel alone, from my cousin's house on the West side to the South side. Often I rode the bus back and forth.

At church I met a woman and her husband who drove me home, once in a blue moon. The wife had a singing group which I joined and enjoyed very much. Then because of my voice people started to notice me.

There was another man who had an attitude, like he thought he was some big wheel, perhaps because he was a preacher. He'd also claimed he was some Bishop's son. In time, he became the pastor. Then when people joined that church, he would have them come to his office where he would talk to them.

Once he told me some mess about me being special, and that he wanted to put me on the air, because of my singing. Back then, he appeared to be in his thirties, which to me seemed old. Yet he strutted around like a peacock; but I soon found out, he was a predator.

He was married, and his wife would disappear from church. Then the peacock would be left for the younger men to drive around, because they seemingly always did his bidding. Well, one evening after church he had his young goons drive me home.

He rode in the car also, and got out, supposedly to walk me to my cousin's door. As I hurried for the apartment, he walked into the courtyard with me, perhaps intending to seem chivalrous for anyone peering out of a window. He also walked me into the lobby. Then before I knew it, this man quickly pulled me under the stairs.

I did not have time to think before he forced himself on me. He pushed me down, and held me there so that he could make me put my mouth on him. He did not care one bit about me crying. All he cared about was himself, and receiving what he thought of as pleasure, at my expense. As he released, he spoke in a low ominous voice. He kept telling me, swallow, as he continued to shove and stab himself at me.

I was so shaken! I was gagging, and I cannot tell you how violated I felt—mostly because I could not tell anyone. I couldn't tell my mother, who was miles and miles away, even though she had tried to protect my sisters from this very thing. I couldn't cry to her, not even on the telephone, because I had no money to call her.

Grieved and alone, I felt I had no one who would feel indignant for me, or who would perhaps even stand up for me. Therefore, again, I wanted to be hidden. As a tall thin growing girl, I often felt alone in the world. I do suppose others looking at me—especially predatory males—could see or sense this. And realizing it, I hated that I couldn't tell anyone!

I especially could not tell anyone at church, because that predator was the pastor! I couldn't say anything at my cousin's home either, because then I would not have been allowed to go to church anymore. Who knows what all else would have happened; and before that experience, church had been my love, my joy, and my solace.

I told you in my prior book that Mother had tried to take us to church wherever we found ourselves. In every state or hamlet that she had moved us to, or fled to, church had been the one constant that she had given us, during my sometimes tumultuous *Seedling* years. We'd moved often, and had run scared, at times as if for our very lives. We'd lived through tornadoes and dust storms in the Midwest. We had been chased by humans, and animals, and other things had truly frightened me. Therefore, church had been a haven for me, and now that vile man had tainted even that!

Oh God, how I cried, hugging all my hurt to my adolescent self, because I felt so alone, and afraid. My eyes also seemingly opened then. Sadly, I saw that there was no protection anywhere for me. I believe that realization pushed me more toward God. I had to wrap myself up in him, because there was no one else. My mother was far away. My step-father E G and pistol-packing little Grandmaw were too. Back then I knew there was no one to come rescue me.

Therefore, I had to depend on God, alone. I remembered Mother's prayers, and how she would sing about stealing away to the savior; and in attempting to do so I cried myself to sleep, many nights.

I must tell you. It is a horrible thing when a woman-child fears nearly everything in her world, when there is no peace, and no solace. It is debilitating when even in sleep, the hurt and anguish experienced are revisited upon one, again and again.

Peacock's Wife

When I could pull myself together enough to re-attend church, the predatory peacock was there, still strutting around like he had never harmed me, or another. How he could do so was beyond me! He even tried to talk to me, but I was wary of him. I stayed away from him, and away from others.

It was a wonder, to me, that no one noticed that I was 'different,' that I now appeared haunted. Often in a quandary, I wondered why me? But I needed to be in church. I needed to be someplace that felt like I could be near the Lord, my only friend. You may wonder why I didn't go to another church. I knew of no others to attend, although there were many.

Jessica Janna & April Alisa Marquette

I happened to see that vile preacher's wife while at church. She was dressed to the nines as usual, but I noticed something more. Her eyes were vapid, devoid of luster and life. After service, she had words for me.

Before the incident, I'd never paid much attention to the woman, but now I recalled having heard that she slept a lot. As she spoke, I noticed her voice too. It sounded dead, lacking vitality, as though her soul had been stolen away, a long time before—most likely due to her husband's antics; or who knows? She too might have suffered as I had. Anyway, predator's wife, whom I now know was clinically depressed, told me, "I know all you little girls think some preacher wants you…"

She went on to state that she was aware that 'we all' wanted her man. That gave me pause, and today it causes me to ask a question. What are girls, or even boys, to do when they cannot tell anyone that they have been violated? What is a youngster to do when they are blamed, for something that should never have been visited upon them to begin with?

When that thing happened to me, in a place deep inside, I became even more fearful than I already was, of men. This, my grown son pointed out to me many years later. And in analyzing that fear, I have realized one thing. When someone foul steals something precious from a youngling, it is devastating. When men, or women, like predator, steal from and prey upon the innocent, they take things from them. In a perfect world, these things should be freely given, at the right time, in loving, nurturing, adult relationships.

In thinking back, I've also realized that if the youngling who was robbed is anything like I was, then that youngster may experience a delayed reaction. For however long, they may not even realize that they have been traumatized. Or they may go a different route. They may become promiscuous, and self-destructive.

Therefore, before *you* judge someone, why not ask yourself: what could have happened to cause that person to 'act out' —as Grandmaw used to say. Ask how you can show them love. Perhaps even request a way, from the Holy Spirit, whereby you may demonstrate patience, because were it not for the Grace of God ... *you* could have had to walk a mile in that person's shoes. You too could have

wound up experiencing the very same thing.

Not So Lovely Memories

After that experience with peacock, others flooded back. I could then see why my mother had kept us moving for the major part of my young life. I understood then, why she'd never wanted men around her girls. It also came back to me, what my father had attempted to do to my older sister. Then I recalled something more...

Back when I'd been a seedling in Arkansas, we'd lived in a shack were the water had sometimes not worked. So after-hours, at the school across the street we pumped it and carried it home.

There was a boy-man –he was not actually any longer a boy, but he was not yet fully a man—who worked at the school. Once when I went to get water, he accosted me, and someone close to our family, of all people, cloaked for him!

I'd buried the fact that as that 'family friend' stood guard so that no one else would see, I'd had to fight, to dig my nails into that boy-man school worker. He fought me too, and managed to get his body fluid on my clean clothing… Those types of things I had shoved deep into my memory bank, trying never to replay any of them. If I'd had a mental vault that locked I'd have thrown those unwanted memories in there.

I'd also have thrown in the memory of another occurrence. Not wanting to, I recalled my stepfather, E G. Once he'd been standing at the woodpile, with some men friends of his. As a seedling, I said something innocuous to him, and he and all the men chuckled. I realize, now, that it had been harmless, but to me, back then, it was hurtful.

I no longer had a father. We'd had to run off from him, therefore, standing there, feeling like my mother's new husband was laughing at me brought all kinds of hurt back.

However, I have since realized that for a while it was easy for me to feel like I was being laughed at, by anyone. I felt that way because precious Mother, who spent a good deal of time trying to protect her children, never allowed us to become close to others, and especially not to men. Therefore, I was caught between a rock and a hard place. I wanted a friend, and a father, but there wasn't one, not for me, not then. There was no one …but God.

Needing to Go Home

Due to all that had transpired, I felt the need to be back in familiar surroundings, so I wound up back in Arkansas, for a visit. I got to see Brother whom I'd taken care of, seemingly so long ago, and I saw Baby Sister who was steadily growing. Although I was happy to be at home with Mother and the family, I found … I no longer really fit.

Therefore, feeling alone, still, and out of sorts, I sought God. I didn't exactly know what all I wanted from him. I did know though, that I had to seek him because I had an inexplicable need, and I desired answers, to unspeakable questions.

Jessica Janna & April Alisa Marquette

While at home, I went to the family church. That was again a pleasure. However, it seemed as if my place was now in Chicago, so that was where I traveled back to.

Yet in time, again I went home. Then Mother idly remarked that I would spend a fortune running up and down the road. Hearing that, I felt my heart break. I felt tears inside, because truly then I felt as if I didn't belong anywhere, or to anyone. I also believed no one knew how alone I was. Back then I felt like I had been given away, to my cousin, who had her own family. Further, I felt like I had no place, no where to belong. I almost wondered if Mother and my family loved me, although I knew they did.

Yes I had bouts of self-pity. A few times I even felt like I'd been reared by seemingly unemotional people. I recalled that during my youngest years I had not been hugged a lot and that I'd lived through many changes. Yet, all of this I kept bottled inside – perhaps because back then, it wasn't the fashion to discuss feelings. People didn't go around spewing all. They kept moving and working. They simply strove to make decent lives for themselves.

Yet now I see that it was through those tough times that my faith was forged, it was also strengthened. As I clutched tightly to it, I learned to keep getting up, to keep moving, just like my ancestors before me. And while doing so, I prayed, earnestly, and I sang, even while I was back in Arkansas.

Strange Cuisine

When I told you about my *Seedling* years, I also mentioned Grandmaw's uninspired cooking. Well one of the times when I was back at home and not in Chicago, Grandmaw told me one of her cooking stories...

She said she met a man, an older neighbor who lived up the road a piece, not close, but not far. Now one day while Grandmaw was out, she met this man, on the road. Grandmaw said Neighbor was selling meat, and she purchased some.

Grandmaw also mentioned that she'd not seen her neighbor's wife in a good while. Well, she said she gave that little thought, because she had to get home to cook her meat.

Grandmaw said that some days later, someone mentioned her older neighbor's wife. They said, matter of fact, that he'd killed the woman, and hacked her up—with a kitchen knife!

Seeming very un-impressed, Grandmaw, who had seen, heard, and experienced many things in her life, simply spoke, in thinking aloud. "That must have been a piece of *her* that I bought..."

Grandmaw sighed, and thoughtfully said, "Well, she was a sweet old woman –but boy was she tough!"

Terrible Storms

I remember being in the Midwest, and I remember tornadoes. Often they would start out in the fields. Sometimes a tiny wind would blow up. It would begin to strengthen, picking up leaves, dust, and other debris. Then this wind would spin faster, and get higher. Ominous clouds could be seen too, off in the distance. They would roll in, sometimes very quickly, and if they brought rain, that was no good.

I say so because if the wind that was gaining speed and traction began to blow and whirl hard enough, and if it spun high enough, it would seemingly connect with the billowing clouds in the sky. Then it could, and often did, become a tornado, right before our very eyes. However, if there was rain also, then chances were, we would not see where the whirlwind was. And that was most dangerous. I say so because the next thing we would hear would be a rushing, as if a freight train was upon us –about to mow us down! Unable to see it, experience taught us that the rain-wrapped tornado was within miles or sometimes even feet of us!

The terrifying buffeting wind and the chaos would then cause us to hide in an old car. I know, you're wondering why we would run out of our *home* to ride out a storm in a battered automobile. Well, during my *Seedling* years, our homes were old. Often they were rickety and not storm-worthy or strong. Therefore, since old cars most times had no wheels on them, and since they were heavy, sturdily constructed, and sat low to the ground, we had the best chance of being safe right there.

I tell you, many times in Chicago, and thereafter in my life, I have thought of those storms, the ones remembered from my youth. I've realized that in life I have felt buffeted by unseen forces and raging winds. However, I have always remembered one thing.

My mother prayed. Wherever she was, she prayed; and I told you before, her prayers weren't long, or filled with eloquent words. Little Mother was a woman of very few words, but she knew one thing, that her God would answer her, that He *would* deliver her. That was the seed of faith that she sowed within me. It is the very seed of faith that

I am sowing within you, within your spirit right now as you read this.

Sure, bad things, many tumultuous things, things that have perhaps taken other people from this life, may have happened to you. Yet, you cannot give up. Sure, you can cry, or you may even pity yourself. Perhaps you have bemoaned situations and circumstances. However, you must finally get a hold of yourself, dig deep. Call on the universe's higher power.

So what, you don't know what to say; maybe you haven't even prayed in Lord knows how long, but start. Yes, at the point of your need. Pour your heart out to the Savior, like I did on so many occasions, those times when I felt tearful, alone, and afraid. Or maybe you can sing...

Jessica Janna & April Alisa Marquette

Honeybunch, I have often sung the hymn, *I Must Tell Jesus*. And that has been the truth. I have also experienced another truth. Whenever, I have relinquished bad feelings, just let them go, I could move on, move ahead.

Whenever I have relinquished thoughts of what was once done to me, and by whom, I have gone forward, put one foot before the other. When I've released fear, and allowed myself to remember that I would be cared for, I have received.

Yes, I have gotten beaten down by life, and I've seemingly gotten knocked about. However, I have *also* known love and lasting friendship. I have known joy and laughter. I have not always cried because my heart was breaking. Sometimes I've cried because God was good, because I came through, because I was happy, and because I have actually been adored.

I know that somewhere, at some point I said this already, but I must say it again. Dear baby, when we let go, when we relinquish, we can reap. Forget stuff that's past. Then the storms in your life won't seem so terrible. When you look back, those storms also won't appear to have lasted as long as you thought they did while you were yet in turmoil's midst. Let go, relinquish, and reap. See, feel, and enjoy newness, along with the warm welcome sunshine that appears after every hard rain, every storm.

Jessica Janna & April Alisa Marquette

Soda Fountain

You know that I was becoming a young
woman, and therefore I needed money. So I worked
at a soda fountain, after school. The soda fountain
was in what was then a ritzy neighborhood. There I
served rich kids. A few were brats, others were not.
I remember that when the younglings ordered, I
made vanilla floats—soda drinks. I made cherry
lime rickies and egg creams.

   After school, kids would burst through the
glass doors of the soda fountain and toss their books
on the counter. The air would be filled with their
playful screams and giggles. They would smell of
sweat and bubble gum. I would stand behind what
could only be classified as a bar, and I would 'pull'

carbonated water to fill the glasses in which I made the requested sugary concoctions.

After work I would catch the late bus back to my cousin's home. At a certain time each night the bus stopped running. Therefore I knew I could never miss it, because if I did, I'd have been up the creek, without a paddle! Missing that bus was a fear of mine. How would I get from that ritzy neighborhood, back to where I lived, in the dark cold Chicago night? I had no idea, and I surely did not intend to find out.

In the daytime, when I sat in school, I was plagued by another fear. I did not want the teacher to call on me, not to read aloud. I didn't feel smart, and I did not want anyone to know. Sure, I knew I had a brain, I knew I used it, but I did not believe I was functioning at my full capacity. However, I had not been taught to reach for the stars, a necessity for children. I believe this was why often I tried to blend; to become invisible, although I never could.

Back then, I also felt like I was always hurrying, rushing through life. I rushed to brush my teeth and dress. I rushed to school. I rushed to my little job. I rushed to do a bit of homework. I rushed not to miss the bus. Many nights I forlornly trudged, a solitary figure, through and miles and drifts of snow, just to hurry to my little bed in my cousin's home.

Oh, I didn't tell you. By this time she had tossed her husband out.

He was back and forth though, because of their boys. He yet actively cared for them while she worked, and I do believe that he and my cousin wanted to mend fences. Yet for some reason, the

mending wasn't truly coming along. However, they

did manage to make up enough to produce another

son.

Factory Work

When I got a bit older, I went to work in a factory. I worked there for what seemed like a year. Most likely it wasn't that long though. However, at that time I was not in school. I was in a warehouse where exercise machines were made.

I had been taught to wire and solder metal in small apparatuses that were supposed to reduce people. These doo-dads were in little cases, and had pads attached. People could take these contraptions and place them on different areas of their bodies, to supposedly reduce fat.

Some people strapped these small padded machines on their legs and thighs. For weight loss others strapped them on their arms, but back then I truly believed that only people with money could have afforded such thingamajigs. Others, like those back where I had come from, needed to spend their money on necessities, and not on what they might have considered frivolity or foolishness.

However, the making of those machines just goes to show that even back then people wanted to look good. It was at this time that I was told, by some, that I should become a model. I must have been a stylish something—although back then, rushing to and fro, I didn't give it much thought.

Working at the factory, I made friends, and once in a while we would go to lunch, to a bar around the corner. In there they had the best food! A time or two, in the evening, those of us from the factory also went to a steakhouse. We were coerced to treat ourselves, and were those steaks great—and tender too! A woman could have probably enjoyed them with no teeth—*or* with her dentures out.

It was at this time that I bought myself a deep blue dress. It was the first real thing I'd purchased, and in the shop, the saleswoman told me that I should become a model. Of course I said something to the effect that I was too tall and the saleswoman argued saying that I was not particularly tall. She gestured, advising me to take a walk with her. She said, "I want to show you a tall girl." And she did.

I wore my lovely new blue dress when I went home. But before I did, I splurged and bought myself a nice pair of shoes, and the shoe saleswoman—one with a big voice—eyed me. As I paraded before the mirror in that shoe, loudly she spoke. "Now that there is a leg!" Oh did she make me laugh. I tell you, I believe that was the time that I slowly began to come into my own. I was blossoming, into a woman.

A few young men had even begun to like me. It seemed they had always been there, but I never really paid them much attention. Maybe that was due to all the shock and trauma I'd experienced in my life. It seemed that when young men asked me to attend dances or parties, I felt ambivalent. Unlike other girls, I could take or leave social affairs, the affairs at which my cousin and her Girlfriend (the one whose husband attempted to force himself on me) were often chaperones.

Of course there were any number of other males who attempted to get me into situations, and into their cars or beds. Sure, they used flattery and soft words, but I can honestly say that I knew none of all that so-called 'sweet talk' would lead to any great love affair. So perhaps being a romantic— without knowing it—I sidestepped, and steered clear.

However, if I was ever out at night I did not forget that I was by myself. I was all too aware that anything could accost me, a dog, a boy, a man… and I did not feel safe, at all. But I needed the little money that I was making, and since I'd not been raised to mooch, I knew I couldn't live on my cousin for free. So I rushed through darkened streets. With my head down, trying to breathe despite the cutting Chicago cold, I hunched over and forged on. Many a night I huddled into my coat that had been a gift from someone who saw that I needed it. With wild winds whipping and howling all around, I raced to relative safety.

Returning To Education

As the days and months passed, I found time to squeeze in school work, and I rushed to my job because those were things I had to do. I realize, now, that Mother had bred tenacity in me, although at the time I did not think about it. I only knew that I had to keep moving, I had to do what I needed to; and I knew that like my mother, I could not stand still.

Often Grandmaw's words, the meaner ones floated back to me. I never forgot that she'd said that I had *an old piece of wore out mammy...* Often that rang in my ears. I remembered that she'd said that *I would do nothing but grow up and bring Cleo a pack of babies...* Those things and others of the like served to keep me on my toes, to keep me moving, because I had to prove Grandmaw and other naysayers wrong.

By this time, my sister, had become a teacher. Remember, she'd been the one whom my cousin initially asked for, to keep her young children. Sister, who was married, and a young mother, would sometimes help me financially so that I could visit home. I did so once when she graduated from the University that had been called AM&N. Dr. Martin Luther King, Jr. appeared to deliver the commencement address, and what a stir that caused!

He was a young man, handsome, and eloquent with words. He held us, his commencement exercise audience, entranced. In his speech we were reminded, that we *would* become something, and that *we* were as special as everyone else that God had created.

After my sister's graduation I returned to Chicago. When I arrived, I found that other relations had taken up residence at my cousin's home. Perhaps they were supposed to help supplement the rent. Maybe they just needed a place to stay for a while…I do not know.

Things were okay, for a time, but of course, the others began their stuff. They started trying to use up all of my and Cousin's toiletries. I guess they didn't want to buy any, or perhaps they didn't have money. Whatever the case, when we'd had enough, Cousin and I ganged up on one male relation. In a huff, we took our stuff back, and boy what a sense of empowerment I felt! Standing up for myself sure was nice.

Then of course, the time came when I had to bid Cousin, and her four sons, farewell... Yes, she had four boys when I finally tearfully left! Although I felt sad at leaving them, for me, life had changed. I felt there were meaningful things that I needed to do, so I journeyed back to Arkansas.

Determined to continue my education, I finished my last year of high school and graduated. Then I started running around on the college campus. Like my sister before me, I started at the university.

During my time at home, eating Mother's good cooking, I gained weight. Then little lithe Ms. Cleo my mother said, "Girl, we have got to get this weight off you," and we did.

Those were some of the best times. It was an exciting period. Everyone my age was preparing to go to, or they were in college. It was what was done in my southern community. Young people readied themselves for study, or to become doctors and teachers. Although Jim Crow was yet in effect, many were excited about burgeoning careers that were opening up to us as young colored people.

Back at the family church the parishioners wanted me to sing…. It was shortly thereafter that I really started working with the children's choirs. Because the gift of song was within me, I was not fearful in that area. It was why I also began to work with the other age-category church choirs. Then I branched out to work with the district and the state choirs. I directed, and sang and travelled with members of our congregation, young and older, and was actively involved in tent revivals. We were all happy to work in conjunction with our dynamic pastor.

During this period, Pastor and older members of our congregation took the young people on many a trip. Riding in a caravan of cars, or a few times on the church bus, the saints drove the younglings to national meetings. These were a gathering of those from the households of faith located in every corner of the country. We met in one central place to worship and fellowship together, and it was exciting! It was eye-opening to see that there were people from all walks of life who believed as we did. In those meetings, some of which were the Sunday School Conventions, and the YPWW [Young People's Willing Worker] conventions, I got to see many a church great.

I will never forget seeing the distinguished spiritual leader, the Apostle, Charles H. Mason, or 'Dad Mason,' as he was often called. He was what is now known as the *first* Presiding Bishop of the Church of God In Christ, Inc. I was awed by that paragon—slight in stature—the patriarch of the church, who walked and prayed. A quiet man, Bishop Mason was highly imbued with the presence of the Holy Spirit, so much so that grace and an otherworldly power emanated from him.

During that time, traveling with church members, at our Pastor's behest, so that we might learn of the Lord and His ways, and His purpose for our lives, we the younglings were taught to fast and pray. We were taken to nearby Memphis, Tennessee, where I also sat in awe at seeing and hearing the renowned songstress, Madam Earnestine Washington. She was the wife of one of the greatest orators of our time, Bishop Frederick D. Washington. Oh, were those the days! Although America was in turmoil, the presence of the Lord prevailed, and it became more evident to me, that I wanted, even needed, to know this God who had been a bulwark and a refuge for my people, and others, for centuries.

Back at the home church, many of the young people that I'd known showed up. It was then or thereabouts that I was asked to lend my voice for radio announcing. I did that for the church broadcast…and thinking about it, now I realize— Lord, that was a *lifetime* ago!

Some of those I knew thought I was special because I had nice clothes. Although no one was aware, some of my clothing I'd painstakingly made. I'd I received some of Mother's talent, her penchant for making clothing and being creative.

All this took place during the time of the American Civil Rights sit-ins. Stand-ins were also prevalent, with some events taking place at the college at Little Rock. It was a time of uproar. Policemen bullied people, and we sat huddled around radios, or before a neighbor's television set, to follow the story of Miz Rosa Parks who'd

refused to go to the back of the bus as 'coloreds'
were expected to do then.

I enrolled in Beauty College (it's called
'cosmetology' now) while I also worked in the
ministry. As more and more people heard me sing
and enjoyed the choirs under my tutelage, it was
said more than once that I should have been on wax.
This meant that I should have been recording, or my
voice should have been on an album, for people to
hear at their leisure.

Once when a bishop said this before a national
congregation of church goers, there were those who
inevitably became jealous. Sure, some people tried
to tear me down with words. However, I kept doing
what I did, because quite frankly, I had heard
meaner words many times before, sometimes even

from my little pistol packin' Grandmaw. Therefore, some of the time some of that stuff rolled off me, like water off a duck's back.

In Beauty College I excelled and received my cosmetology license, perhaps because doing hair appealed and came naturally to me. I loved learning, and beautifying others.

My Own Moving & Shaking

Despite all that I was doing, I had a feeling inside… It felt like I was soon supposed to be elsewhere, doing something altogether different, something more. So I prayed.

Sometimes when others were eating, I fasted, as we'd been taught, at my family church. I sought to know God's will for my life, and I believed I would go on, maybe move to another state, but not back to Illinois. That life was done.

Then the feeling became stronger as the days passed, and like the mover and shaker that Mother had once been, I knew that I too would have to get in the wind. I prayed because I knew that I would leave Arkansas. I had no idea where I would go, at first, or how I would get there. I only knew and believed that God's Holy Spirit would lead me.

And He did! I became aware that I would go to New York. It was crazy! Yes, from a natural non-spiritual standpoint because I knew no one there. Yet I'd heard about wealthy people who were hiring household help.

When some in my church found out about my aspirations, they and others told me I couldn't make it there—no, not in *New York*! Perhaps these people were well-meaning. Perhaps they believed I should stay where I'd seemingly begun to build something. Or maybe the truth was they too wanted out. It could have been that they were jealous that I could leave them behind. Others were openly hurt.

Children were bewildered and wondered why I wanted to leave.

The truth is I didn't so much *want* to go. I loved the choirs, and the little ones. Yet I felt as though I was continually being pulled away. I now know that I was being *called*, by the Holy Spirit. I told you in my first book, *Seedling*, which details my youngest years, that I always knew I would leave Arkansas. Even as a small girl, I knew it, deep within. At the time that I was embarking upon, and thinking about leaving, I had no idea that it was the chosen path for my life. I simply knew that I had always desired a different type of life.

I then began to embrace the feeling that I was being led to New York. As a young woman, with no money to speak of, I prayed and told Spirit that if this was truly for me to do, then to please provide. That was the only way I could go, because I had no connections, and as far as I knew, there would not even be a job waiting for me.

Yet I had to take steps of faith. I had to prepare myself, mentally. I began packing, silly that it seemed. I moved in the belief that the Holy Spirit would make the way clear. And He did!

With reference to those job openings I'd heard of, a few teachers, young women who also desired to do and experience different things, made plans to go. Some of them I knew from when I'd been an adolescent. These women and I viewed the job openings as a way to make money over the summer, while experiencing things that we previously had not. I was going one step further though. In simply following the leading of the Holy Spirit, I wanted to see where I would wind up.

And so I was off… The teachers and I left, on a Greyhound bus. Mother cooked and sent food with me. In my mind it is all very hazy now, since these evens took place 50 some odd years ago, maybe more. Yet I do remember that I was excited!

My Thoughts

There is a song, one that I love. It was recorded by the late Reverend James S. Cleveland. In it he sings: *if anyone should ever write my life story...* He says that through every line written, there would be one constant —*Jesus, He Is the Best Thing*... that ever happened...

I too say the same thing. I tell you truly, most of my life I felt like I was on the run. Sometimes things were hard, and sometimes situations were sad. Other times there was wonder and joy, and now that I am no longer a seedling, or a youngling, I still feel as if I'm running—although quite a bit slower. However, I'm running for good, not attempting to escape someone or something.

I've said it before. Sometimes I've felt I was born on the move. Those of you who read *Seedling* my youngest years, are aware that my mother was constantly in motion. Therefore, movement just might be in my blood. Throughout all the movement however, there was guidance, and wisdom, from above. God most assuredly gave me to know when to move—many times out of harmful situations, other times He directed me *not* to move. Then I simply had to wait.

Amid all those occurrences, even when I felt as though I

journeyed alone, I held fast to my
faith. I sought God again and again.
I believe I was like David, the
Bible's Psalmist. Before things
failed, or when all else failed, I
turned to God, and it has been His
presence that has carried me.

Sure, I have had to cry, and sure
I wanted stability; but then again,
had I received all I wanted, I would
not have this particular story to tell.
Therefore, I am grateful. I have
learned, and am yet learning, to

quit looking back. No regretting
things that are behind; for there is
nothing past that can now be
changed. I simply accept that this is
my life, the one that I was given.
And with it I choose to do what I
have often heard in a little saying. It
goes: *the best thing that you can
do with a life is give it away...*

So my dear, in doing just that, I
have and will continue to give you
what I have received. I hope that
after learning my story, you will be

blessed, surely as blessed—or more so than I have been.

Oh, and let go. If you can get past hurt and trauma, if you can forgive, or if you are simply *willing* to forgive, the Holy Spirit will aid you. He will do the rest. He'll help you with the 'relinquish' part, so that you may reap and so that you can rejoice.

I love you, and pray daily for you. It doesn't matter whether or not I know your name. You still happen to be among the number. You're one of those that I ask God to bless and reveal Himself to when I pray for His people.

Be blessed my dearest,

Jessie

_____*_____

And...for another glimpse into her life, look for:

Yielding
Jessica Janna
&
April Alisa Marquette

Non-Fiction

The **3rd** install in the
Relinquish & Reap Series

Thought provoking and poignant...you may laugh or cry as you look into Jessica's life.

One of six purse-sized books offering practical wisdom; each will feel as if a lovely friend is telling you her irrepressible story. She is quite simply...buoyant!

Then— Jessica's seventh, an engrossing full-sized volume, will tie all together...

Yielding
The 'Becoming' Years

Jessica Janna
&
April Alisa Marquette

A newly blossomed young woman, again Jessica winds up far from home. Now she is in New York, this time even farther away from all she's known.

In her life however, there is one constant – change. Amidst, she meets people, from many different walks of life. Among them there is a man, the one that she will ultimately marry…

Yielding, is the **third** account in Jessica Janna's optimistic, true-life inspirational *Relinquish & Reap* Series.

Desire good fiction?

Glimpse the character inspired by **Jessica Janna**.

Read about *the priestess*, and Aqua-- In the
mysterious, erotic, supernatural thriller...

Exodus
by
April Alisa Marquette

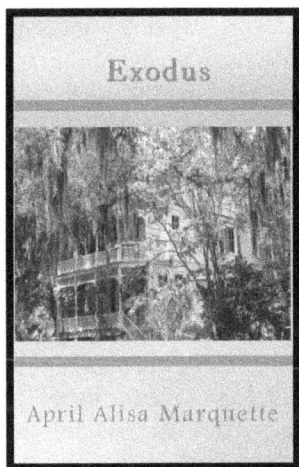

Enjoy the following excerpt:

THAT night Aqua left Noel's bed. Amid incessant whispers urging her on, she floated, up the small narrow staircase, to the third floor bath.

This time the door was not stuck. Partially open, familiar children's laughter floated out.

It seemed she had heard the airy giggles many times before. But hadn't … she—or someone, *killed* the children?

As she glided forward, her feet never seeming to touch the floor, Aqua's heartbeat quickened. With her hand on the brass knob, she peered inside, and saw two golden haired babes. Perhaps they were three year-olds, but they could have been four.

They had halos of spiral curls; and splashing and laughing, their little faces beamed like sunshine. Their Butter-colored skin was smooth, stretched taught over curvy little arms, legs, and unblemished backs.

When they turned their heads, yet giggling, Aqua saw their little button noses and lush lips.

Then one child pivoted to look at her, and Aqua wondered, where these children bi-racial? Slowly, the other child also faced her, and she squinted. What color were their eyes?

They were…amber. No green. Wait. Were they gray?

Unable to tell, Aqua moved forward. Suddenly she screamed, and backed up, because the children's eyes were actually hollowed-out sooty *sockets*!

Tickled at her distress, the little ones turned, to face away…

Exodus...

Available NOW
April Rain Books

www.aprilalisamarquette.com
Barnesandnoble.com
Amazon.com
Books-A-Million

Jessica Janna & April Alisa Marquette

———————— * ————————

Then…

April Alisa Marquette does it again…

If you enjoyed visiting The Isle and meeting the High Priestess, in Aqua and Noel's tale —*Exodus* then take a trip.

Rejoin the priestess, and those surrounding her, in the lush, sensually mysterious and supernatural:

Affinity

The second install of the *Sea Isles Series* –a trilogy that is not to be missed.

Bon Voyage!

www.ingramcontent.com/pod-product-compliance
Lightning Source LLC
Chambersburg PA
CBHW020949030426
42339CB00004B/24